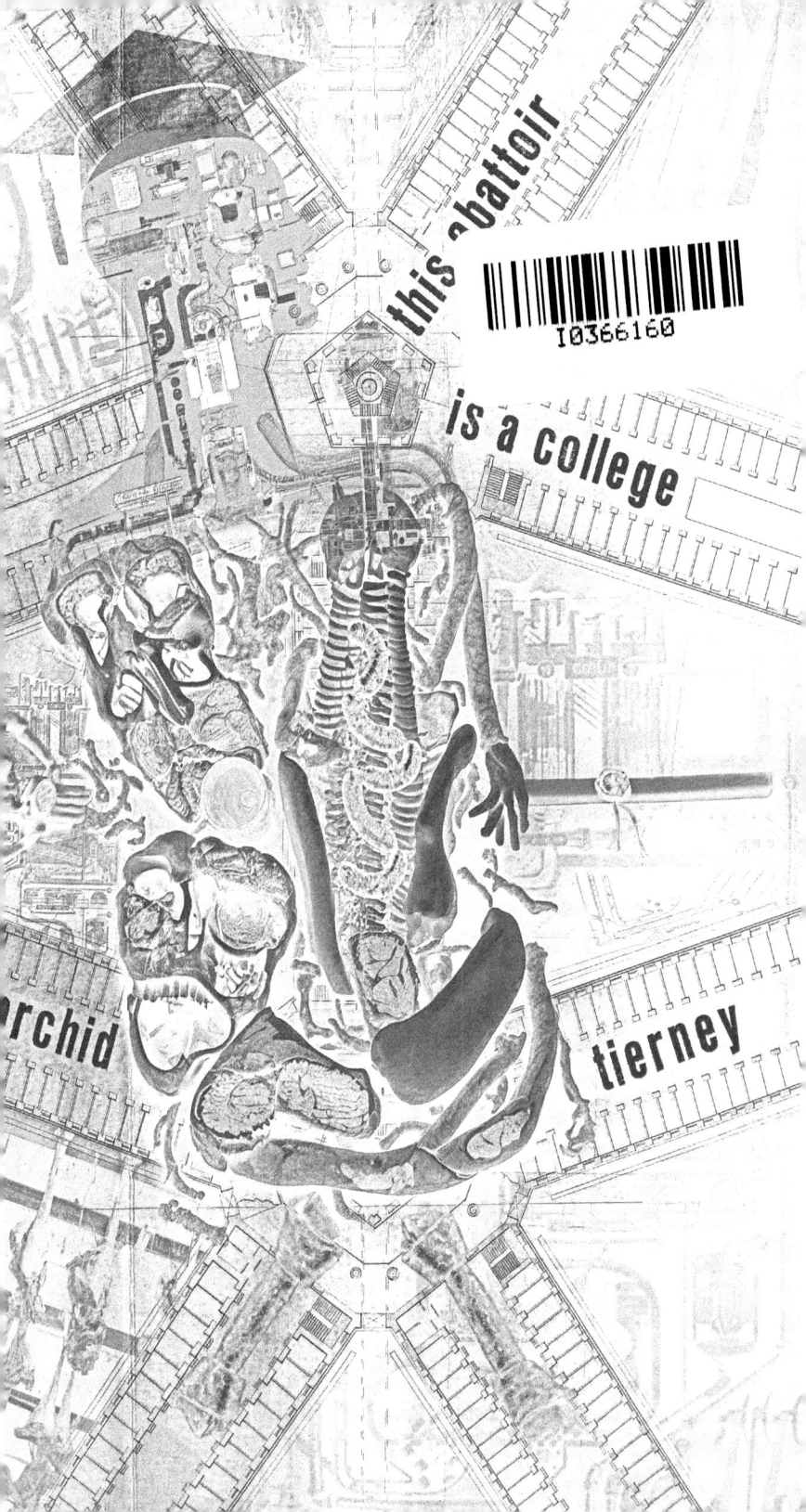

this abattoir is a college
orchid tierney

ISBN 978-1-940853-39-0

◎ 2025. All rites reversed.

This book may be freely reproduced, adapted, repurposed, etc., as long as it is under these same copyleft conditions (not to be copyrighted or reproduced for commercial gain).

published by Calamari Archive
NY, NY

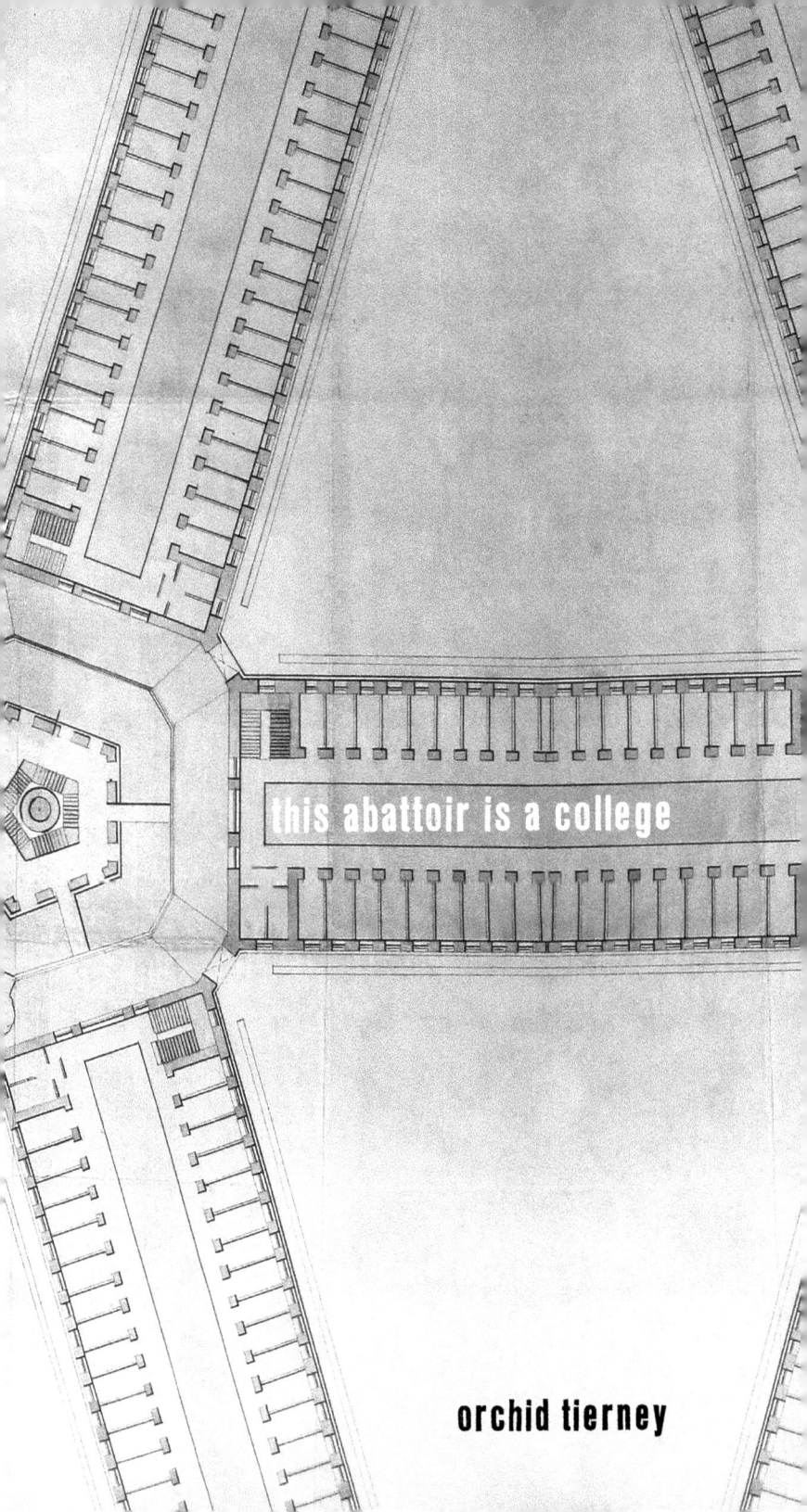

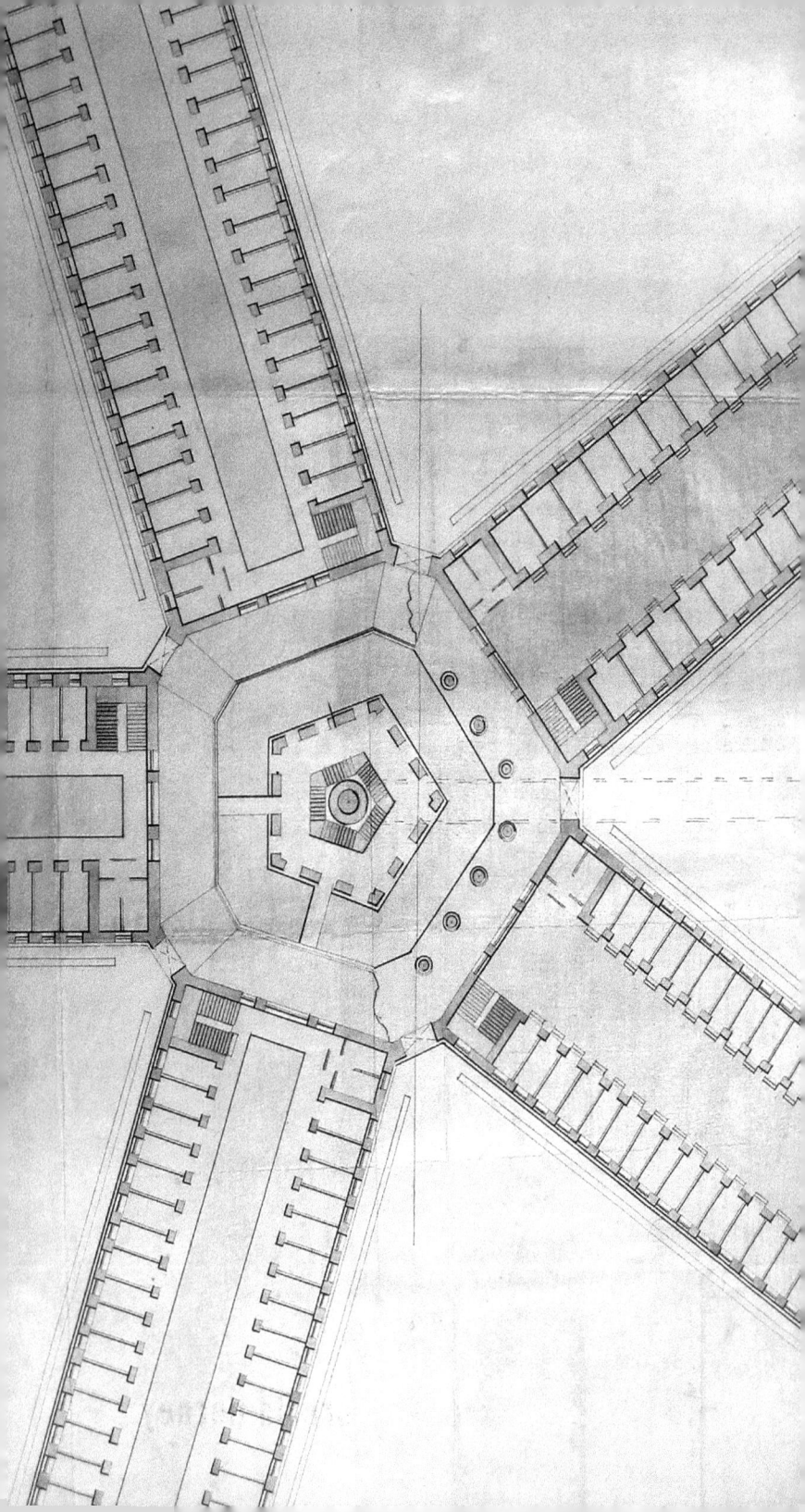

belongs to s.b., j.g., c.b.,
and all future thinkers

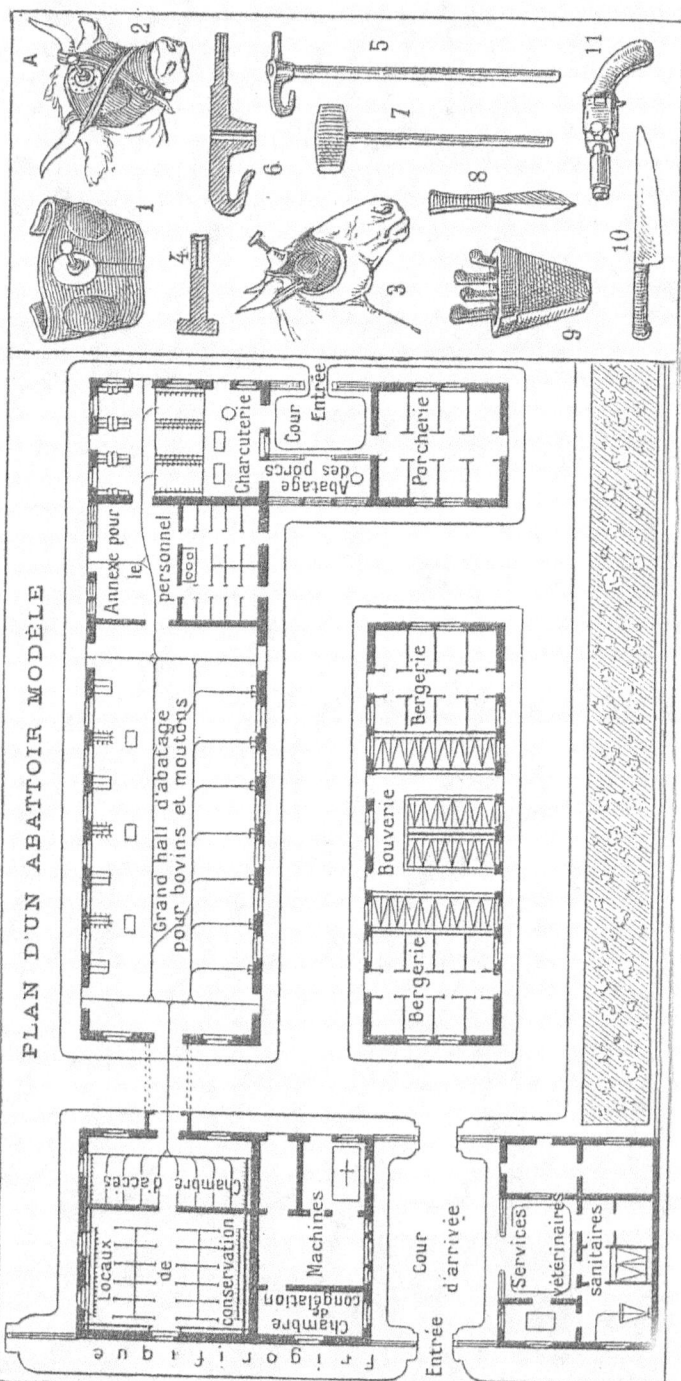

PLAN D'UN ABATTOIR MODÈLE

this is a house of

design	9
disappointment	35
desire	63
cartload	92

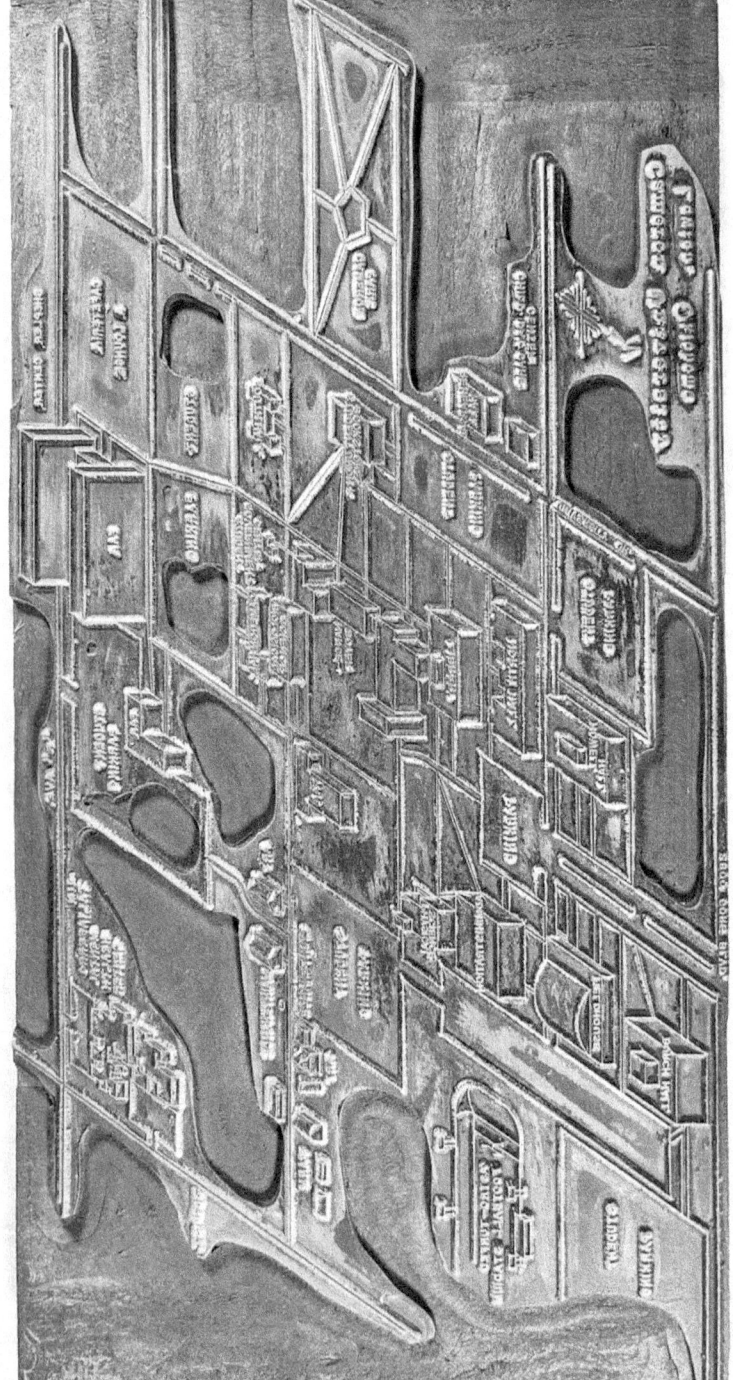

design

When the cattle are raised right, they have a really good life.
> —Temple Grandin
> "Temple Grandin on Autism, Death, Celibacy and Cows"

[S]ometimes you do get attached to the lambs, especially the orphans. But you get over it. They're not pets, they have to make their living.
> —Charlotte Grace
> "From school to the slaughterhouse"

a slaughterhome for a reputable killer

necropastoral

when the line is a city. it is a narrative for mourning. the first half of the sun is grit. the second promises a difference. the city is a factory for organising indifference.

what does not change is the will to change says Olson.
this line needs further inquiry.

a line is a city with a meatpacking district. this space is a lattice of red brick and grey beef. a cover of clover and cleaver. for monkey calves. and paper sheep. units are sent here for slaughter. design is a difference that measures the distance.

a ghost house spites the banks of a hidden holy river. a spectre of dread. the zombie of toil. this is a century. that calls itself dust. callouses that dress for a silent market. a reputable killer refuses to handle. this slaughterhome is a murder. a cocoon for cows and colleagues. a community of corses. a dead zone for the living. a line for a factory. an assembly of faculty. choice is a word and a killing floor. the slick of animal matter. thick sticks. and battery acid. the street is electric with spasms. the corner chafes the difference between sweetness and crunch. trains that sting with cattle and kin. skins and limbs. loins and shins. here is a swill of bite. and beer. a stock of GREs. a grave of SATs. a chain of flesh and candy. sugar and blood. this mundane world. is grace and slaughter.

bricks. wood. candy. hooves. tests. beers. this stranger engrained on a Polaroid photo. a murmur. a memory. a history of waiting. and in the frame the units whisper. *everyone must make their living.*

a stanza is a standing place

a house. a slaughterhome. a stanza. tenders the living. udders a stall. for assembled units. a narrative is one sentence that must follow another. a line a machine for managing. infinity.

Limpet is a knocker and a narrative. not a sticker or brainer or splitter or butcher or inspector or driver or dean or president or farmer or administrator. Limpet labours in a living room. a house of laughter. a home is a job and a killing floor. a spray of compressed air and matter. dampened with sweat. exhaust and methane. compacted in tension. here is a cage for dismembered inquiry. a stall is suspense. uneasy in waiting. a narrative for organising silence. here is a classroom for pairing and sharing. a one-minute paper. a whiteboard for inhuman feeling. units eel through the chutes like hard water. tourists move in. organs move out. a list of conditions a promise. putrescence and pleasure.

if bones are sentient. if bible is conscious. if rumen is ruminating. if maw is divining. if bonnet is honeycomb. if brain is battery. the difference is glutinous. then doorways to heaven. then cruelty of assessment. then inquiry is guck. and stupid. and useless. here is a spray of slime and crime. this question is grotesque and brainless. even the narrative is splitting.

a unit is a drift of animal organs

this is the unit's eighth attempt to write this novel.

a unit is a tourist. a cow. a commodity for slaughter. this unit writes ramps then corrals then doorways then heavens. a narrative is a plot of productive land. a plot is a field waiting for narrative. to narrate is to count. to count is to drill for a character's fault. this fault is a line is a hole to drive the narration. narration is an account. the account is a bank. and bunk. and gunk. and useless. this is a precise mathematical repetition. the plot is a field. then a system. an enclosure. the brain is the same to the liver and shin. a skip. a tumble. a stammer. a stumble.

to unplug the drain, the unit revises its story. first as a novel. then as a prayer. if novel. not a poem. if prose. not a letter. a missive and a mission. a thesis and theatre. *the goal of the reader is to read beyond the page* says Samuels. the unit remembers this productive lesson. a legend. a lesion. the unit's goal is a list of mischief. to imagine the margins. the inscriptions. the proscriptions. the prescriptions. the misfit tends to the plot on the table. to unclog. debrain. to flush the toilet. the unit rewrites this line. this line. this line. this line. this line. then another. and another. the novel detaches in fragments.

the novel is gender. and genre. it is a kind. a kin. a cow. a capital slaughter. one line is rung. one rung is for ruin. another for tenure. *is this a sermon or a poem* wonders the unit. *a collage or a college.* the sentences are suspended. each line is taut. a muscle in rigor. a corpse. a corse. skeletal segments grainy with anticipation. a photo. a frame. linty particles for thinking. when each line is a hook. the text hangs like a carcass transferred from the slaughter. this line is bare offal. this sentence is tripe. this syntax is tongue. these words are spleen. beautiful organs are drawn to the dinner table.

this is a house not lived in

Limpet labours in a sweet house of desire.
this house is an abattoir. a college. a clean institution.

this college is a settler. this college is a committee.
this college is a machine for war and policing.

Limpet is a bulldozer. a system. a knocker.
a commodity. a product. a unit. a resource.
and a head.

Limpet knocks to the beat of a pneumatic gun.
Limpet is tender. viscid. and sticky.

narrative is a lorry.

outside the northwester wind is calcareous and chalky.
inside the air is copper and ferric. captive penetration.
compact air. a lesson. or lesion. a legend. allusion.

a straight line of organs stuns a serpent of products.
bolt guns. magenta. weird tungsten. strange sunlight.
Limpet is lifeless. a vassal. a vessel. a stall. a pen. a
body erect.

a floor. a swing. a swig. a glint of light unsure of its
inflection. here is a space to tender reflection.

during long hours. he narrates the space between his
brain and the liver.

sometimes he is stern. at times he is joyous.

an udder day. an udder dollar.
he accuses. alleges. and confuses.

what do you call a barrel upon a cow's head.
Limpet things a thought. haha. a capital joke.

tones in the air. heretics on paper. a listless limb. cruel but forgiving. a hoof. a gun. a fall. a knife. a swing. a swig. a glint. a body in motion.

this text hangs like a caress.
this text hangs like a carcass.

what this beauty is. this stanza in the liver.

a sentence is a unit in artificial tension

this is the unit's eighteenth attempt to write this novel.

each sentence is a product. each line is suspension. each stanza is resource. each liver is fever with imprisonment.

the unit is obsessive. rewrites the same sentence.
one line after another.
one sentence after another.
one stanza after another.
one liver after another.
a sentence is a unit in artificial tension.
a unit is intention.
a spell to dislodge the appendix.
a painful light is a slip of the knife.
a serpentine ramp is calming.

useless. tender. viscid. and sticky.
there is a need for further inquiry.
a tubercular whiteness gathers a cloud.
grey matter for capital. chattel for cows.

the unit takes long walks to feel porous and useful.
this unit is a cow. a downer. fit for the slaughter.
one rung on the ladder is for ruin. another for tenure.
a unit is a commodity is a system with purchase.
a sentence is a corral. this line is for profit.
replication is calming. enclosed in the pen.
the unit repeats. the unit recites. the unit renews.
a sentence is a mantra is a prayer. and a unit in tension.

> *a sentence is a unit in artificial tension.*
> *a sentence is a unit in artificial tension.*
> *a sentence is a unit in artificial tension.*
> *a sentence is a unit in artificial tension.*
> *a sentence is a unit in artificial tension.*
> *a sentence is a unit in artificial tension.*

a sentence is a unit in artificial tension.
a sentence is a unit in artificial tension.
a sentence is a unit in artificial tension.
a sentence is a unit in artificial tension.
a sentence is a unit in artificial tension.
a sentence is a unit in artificial tension.
a sentence is a unit in artificial tension.
a sentence is a unit in artificial tension.
a sentence is a unit in artificial tension.
a sentiment is unity in artificial tentacle.
a sentiment is unity in artificial tentacle.

a separation is untruth in artificial terminals.
a sequence is an uprising in artificial terms
a seraph is upstage of the artificial terminus.
a serf is an uprising in artificial territory.
a sergeant is an upsweep in this artificial terror.

design is a method for heaven

in this ferric future the city has six seasons. useful and trussed. clay and rust. gristle and grease. these seasons are tender and molested. each season lasts for a semester. a block. or a quarter.

one week is for lorries to deliver the heads. one semester is for potholes and death. another for carvers and lovers to cleave. one is for bulldozers to build swimming pools. tracks and gyms. grey towers and statues. museums and encampments. one is for curves. and chutes. campuses. IT systems. town and gown planning. one is for doors and classrooms. dorms and dining halls. student centres. lecture halls.

a head is a unit with four limbs and a tail.
a head is a unit with a course schedule.
a head is a unit that jumps over the moon.
a unit is the tune from what the old cow died.
a unit is a transaction. an exchange of services.
a unit is a course credit.
a unit is a product.
a unit is a student and professor. a cow and a calf. a lecturer and athlete. a learner and assistant. a fellow and visitor. a guest and a host. a postdoc and full. a grader and clinician. an auditor and slacker. a TA and associate. a dropout and emeritus. a worker and a boss.
a unit is tenure track and survivor and luck.
a unit is adjunct and surplus and system.
a unit is suspension and a sentence in tension.

a hall of learning is a doorway to heaven

Limpet ferrets Hog. his friend on the classroom floor. he cleaves a story to the tune from what the old cow died. a story is a tree. which is to say it is true. this story is a skeleton that hangs like a caress. that hangs like a carcass.

Temple Grandin Limpet carps Hog *invented the serpentine ramp. this ramp curves with love to mask the view of the cattle.*

and what do the units find at the end of the ramp asks Hog. *blue doors* Limpet replies. this design is useful and calming.

one night when the crew was working late Limpet parrots *I stood on the nearly completed structure and looked into what would be become the entrance to heaven.* at the end of *your* life can *you look back and be proud.*

do you contribute something worthwhile to society Limpet wonders.

does your life have meaning?

monkey calves. paper sheep.
the air is cupric and ferrous.

knock knock. Limpet says.
who's there. the unit replies.

the units have to make their living.

the history of enclosure

history erases a settlement. a useful pasture. a system. a prisoner. a pioneer. a square on a chess board. surface of a shield. a field is disciplinary. a state and a plot. an open country. a plantation. a field is unencumbered by marsh. mountain. hill. forest. and a campus garden.

a college is an enclosure. a tool for abstracting space. a college is a settler. a capital ghost. a by-product that collects its monsters. this college must close. this college will founder. this college will swell with desperation. this college is a prison. a campus for protesting. this college is a farm. husbandry for culling.

the pasture is open. the pasture is tilled. closed fruits for the cutting. a field is a category for knowledge. a field is a silo. a closed writing space. a pen. a parrock. a flowerbed. a park. a spill of new money. patties in stupor and legacy until free to wander. grass wheat. a middle-class lawn. a fence transforms the waste land into a campus. mascot clovers. who are cleaved to be cleft. a field is a medium. a telephone. a computer for cataloguing. grief and chattel.

the field is arable. grazed. gazing. murals and music. language and art. that field is useless. this field is useful. that field is for profit. this field is genocide. that field is rhetoric. this field is employment. that field is internship. this field is credentialed. that field is theory. this field is craft. that field is contemporary. this field is history. that field is modern. this field is superstition. that field is chemistry. this field is mathmatics. that field is philosophy. this field is physics. that field is poetry. this field is drama. that field is finance. this field is management. that field is language. this is the only real field of action.

the college is a managed pastoral

the players are iron.

Limpet is a knocker.
Hog is a butcher.
cow is kyne. is kin. is kind. is cadaver. is a useful machine.

a cow is most accomplished when it is cold.

what's the use asks Ahmed. a use is a queer tool for creating.

Limpet watches the lorries arrive. watches them depart. examines his fingers. explores his limbs. inspects his mouth. dry bones a dip on his tinder. a tongue. inspects his eyes. a painful light is a slit of the knife. checks his knife. his hands. his bank account. his stomach is capital. a tubercular whiteness. taps his ears. milks his lips. capitalism produces nature.

Tenure / is terror writes Silliman.
does your life have meaning?

an abattoir is a breach in the wall. a difficult hunger. the narrative is cow. thus chattel. thus capital. thus a sentence at the doorway to heaven.

Hog watches Limpet watches the lorries watch the cows watch Limpet watches the fields watch the cows watch the knives trade in teeth. Hog slices Limpet with stomachs.

a stomach is indignation. disgust. disappointment. and four chambers.

teeth are a collection of truths. appreciation. and care.

stomach says Hog *is stress. all animals deserve humane treatment. to tender the meat.*

teeth says Limpet *is deed. a flexing tendon umbrellas the air. a worker animal. a unit. a touch. a kind.*

stomach. *you can't stop a bull with a poem.*

teeth. *a cow is a historical whole.*

stomach. *prose is a process. a poem is a system. a college is a narrative. a sentence is tension.*

teeth. *cattle are chattel. are capital. are units. are unity. an untidy udder. a worker unit.*

Hog erases poetry. Limpet ignores prose. Hog verbs Limpet. Limpet nouns Hog.

stomach. *isn't [the avant-garde] fundamentally incompatible with assimilation into the academy* asks Golding.

Hog exclaims Limpet. whittles kisses. stuns capital. *that's the hole tooth and nothing but the tooth.*

does your life have meaning?

an abattoir is a breach in the wall. a difficult hunger. two walls made of light. one wall made of paper. another built from beef. one from bubbles. red wheels and feathers. one with lungs and livers. another from manes and mouths.

this design is a courtyard and a pen made of marble. of blood and dung. these cows are systems of water. a bag of organs. blood vessels. a courtyard is a palace or waiting room. a pen is a prison or quill. a slaughterhouse is a castle of glistening machines.

Le Corbusier likens *our eyes are made to see forms in light.*

forms of light useless to bruising. a college of concrete. plastic. and steel. empty space and factories. grand pyramids and murals. aesthetics and visions. a prism of farm labour. bucolic surfaces. engineered rivers. polymer prairies. and effluent gardens. *the Plan [is] the essence of sensation.*

this slaughterhouse is a civilising machine. a combustion engine. a 1908 Model-T. an automaton ghostly with prospect. it is a process and a system of dead labour. a house is a mecha for living in. a slaughterhouse is a narrative and a sentence. a skeleton in verse. an abattoir is a college with units for slaughter. a poem is a house. a stanza a room.

Browne writes *poetry is a window which enables belonging*

a stanza. a slaughter. a breach in the wall. the slaughterstanza for a reputable killer. this is a poet's novel corrected to love. but what about love is novel.

the gravity of inelegant bodies

Limpet is knocking a bobby calf.

knock knock.
who's there.

does your life have meaning?
we have to make our living.

coldness of the killing floor acidic with fatigue. galaxy stares. calloused fingers. a reputable killer. here the units are emergent and tender. o of the gun incurs concretion and pressure. electric with quietude. hippest of pain. a stanza in the liver. a spine is stannous. static on the radio. the ceiling is always ugly at this time of the semester. trussed by the limb. units shoulder third person pronouns. academic wholeness in a collection of parts. an edited volume that sells seven digits. tourists move in. organs move out. Limpet is tender to the head and the heart. soon the knife notches the calendar of bone. here is the tripe. there is the offal. here is battery. there is blood. here is fat. there is heart. *o o o o o.* over time the unit will resemble household items.

a unit asks an invisible question

this is the unit's nineth attempt to write this novel.

even the air is obscene with this pleasure. each word drives the body closer to dismemberment. a sentence transferred to a lorry. transformed into slaughter. is the unit a novelist. an essayist. a server. a poet. is the unit a cow or a house. a student or a professor. is it a lecturer. a counsellor. a resource. a scholar. a worker. a loafer. a guide. a slacker. a manager. a mentor. an advisor. a policeman. a parent. a warmonger. a manager. a friend. a wheel. a collaborator. a flatline. a protestor. a camera. a mother. a wife. an advocate. a maid. a service. a waitress. a mesh. a waste. is this plot a plastic of catalysts. an inciting incident. where is sentiment a threshold. or is it a fault line. or a fruit. spring break. or semester. is this narrative a college. or sickness. does the unit reproduce. unity through conformity. is the unit tired. or a downer. is the unit cruel and useless. or capital and useful. must the unit write a paragraph to advance to an ending. to construct blue doorways to heaven. does engendering the novel answer the downer's last question. *how is a sentence a wall.* is a doorway an exception. a commodity for tenure. a capital idea. the answer is yes. the answer is no. yes and no. yes and no. and maybe. the novel's bureaucracy transforms the text into a graduate programme.

what's the use

to use is to enjoy to observe and to manage to handle to have sex with control. *use is radiant with desire.* if use is a hand it is a blacksmith's mad arm. to madden is to queer. to queer is to foreign. to foreign the arm is to make it fragile. Limpet lusts fingers flexed with and fission.

Limpet is knocking a unit. a shiver. a shake. *to make this assignment* work *we ought to assign page limits* he muses.

the history of [a] *school system is the history of machinery* replies Ahmed.

Hog fervently disagrees. *to make the assignment work* he argues *we must assign page limits*.

this job is a mass and a cartload of manure. a piece of work and stock. used until exhaustion. Limpet is depleted. even his uselessness has a history of extraction.

yes yes yes. the units sing in buzzing unison. *we agree with the user. to make this assignment work we must assign a page limpet.*

Limpet starves the professor into a docile relation. he vanishes into his fingers. he turns into a template. he wets into womanhood. she is furious and female. her use is a bleed. his use is expulsion. her expulsion is male. he bleeds into the doorway.

this abattoir is a college

an assortment of buttons

between the bolts Limpet crows out a taxonomy.

a cow is a button he bleeds to Hog.

a cow is a plastic bag. shampoo and conditioner. polyester jacket. fabric softener. personal computer. condom. crayon. steering wheel. lipstick. candy floss. prep test. punctured tire left on the curb. dictionary cover. librarian. briefcase. university diploma. tambourine. pencil. toothpaste. adjunct. moisturizer. china cup. car seat. pen. fire extinguisher. fellow. dorm room. glue stick. shaving cream. blue book. emery board. plywood. wallpaper. visiting professor. photographic film. desk. guitar string. tennis racket. anti-aging cream. student. telephone wires. textiles. lecturer. antifreeze. foundation. fertilizer. matches. custodian. fireworks. chalk. paint. administrative assistant. insulation. grader. perfume. deodorant. brush. felt. timepiece. gardener. plaster. biodiesel. blue books. maintenance worker. charcoal. athlete. white and brown sugar. glass. HEPA air filter. classroom. water filter. gummy bear. dean. chewing gum. plastic bottle of vegan dishwashing liquid. admissions building. professor. pine-scented washing detergent. custodian. cat food. dog food. work study intern. cement. drum kit. hormone replacements. vitamins. comb. eyeliner. pen holder. shoe glue. teaching assistant. brake fluid. nail polish. varnish. research agenda.

a sentence is a cooling room

these sentences will form a sanctuary for refusal writes Gladman.

a system of opening and closing that both isolates them and makes them penetrable encloses Foucault.

or a sentence is a system of hygiene. or a motion in space. or a space in crisis. or an accumulation of calamities. or a sentence to break. or a hole to seal. or a line is a system in planning. a print. a blueprint. a blue door to college.

a pedagogy of disappointment

twilight is a walking ghost. a house is a palace for farm animals contained in refrigerators. transcripts in garages. classrooms. test preps. anatomies. GREs. SATs decorate the white walls. common apps. cover letters. syllabi. policies. diplomas. cattle. transcripts. chattel. capital. broken bottles on the edge of a kitchen sink.

carnivorous sacrifice is *vital to modernity* says Derrida.

what worlds are beauty when *we* are incompatible with life.

the useless mouths

Limpet eats straw. he feels *weak as a woman*. he lives like a cow. he is hungry. is crisis. he is a designation called useful. who must die. who is useless. he is a pronoun driven into foul ditches.

what kind of worker are you asks Hog.
dying. Limpet cries. *in* this *economy?*

he is a wife. she is a downer. and a haunt. his skin is clammy with famine. the moon is black in the fosse. the bones are wet with women. tourists move in. organs move out. in death *you* will steal his moo.

mad cow

what if *we* are incompatible with light. Limpet holds up his tote bag with his debut cover reveal. *this unit is a professional poet* he tells Hog. he is appearances versus unreality. all he has a mug with his face. a book launch and a dream. buy his merch. press like. click to subscribe.

please tell the unit how to read Stein Hog demands. or begs. or pleas. the units are burdened with their cave-in sagas.

read her like injury the bulldozer replies. a stanza in the liver. then *one sentence after another.*

Hog nouns a unit. Hog verbs his friend. they close their eyes. they shape the slaughterhouse into a campus. their words build swimming pools. tracks and gymnasiums. football fields. scoreboards. admission buildings. parent outreach. alumni networks. financial aid offices with elevators that take years to reach each floor. they spin syntaxes and prefixes. gerunds and pluperfects. subjunctives. continuous presents. they are creating perfect futures.

their dreams have stuttered. a unit succumbs. Hog and Limpet open their eyes. they reappear on the killing floor between carcasses and candied flesh. blood drains into a gutter.

what is this Hog snorts. *an english department?*

disappointment

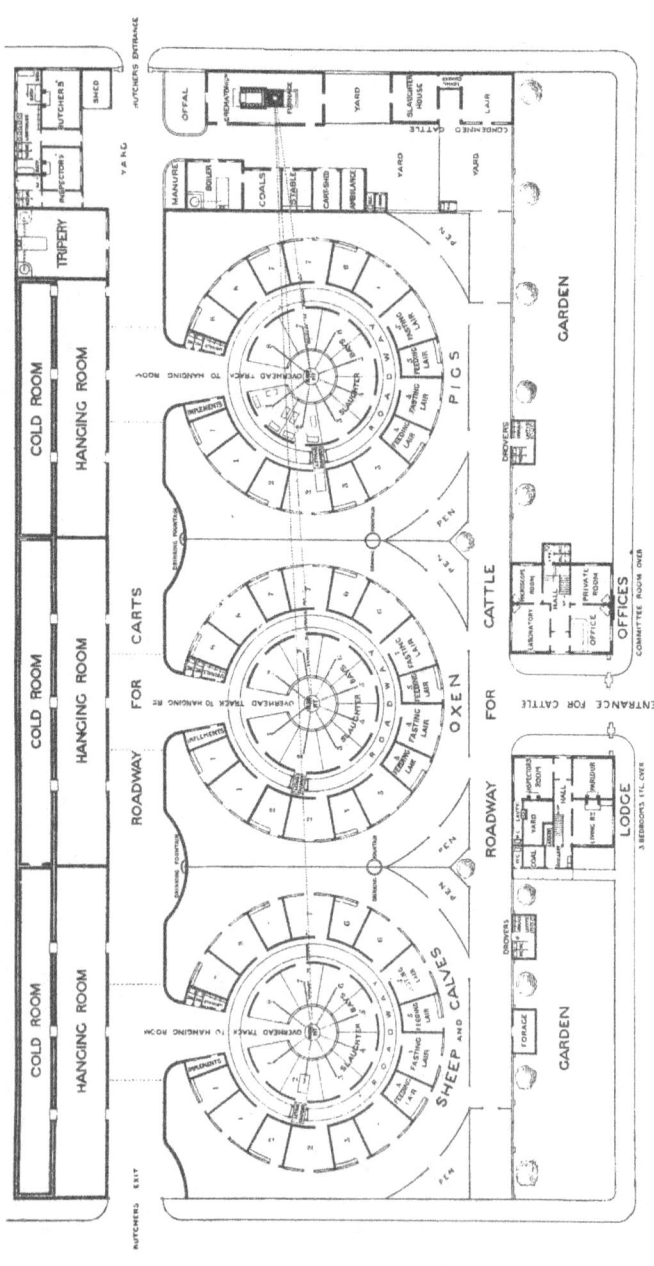

"...slaughterhouses 'must be solid and no more, in order to avoid high costs, and they must be completely removed from all ambitions to architecture and ornamentation.'"
      —Ministry of Interior
      quoted in Paula Young Lee,
      "Siting the Slaughterhouse:
      From Shed to Factory"

The Committee recommends that the principal characteristics of a factory abattoir should be single control, specialisation of labour, continuous process, the killing being spread fairly evenly over at least four days of the week, and a uniform condition and appearance of the finished product in place of the variations at present existing in the condition not only of the meat but also of the by-products. The Committee prefers a multi-floor factory abattoir to the single floor type found in nearly all the public abattoirs in England, on grounds both of hygiene and economy.
      —"Abattoir Design"

...the human ensemble is
a compound mechanism and process
immeasurably superior
in designing nicety
      —R. Buckminister Fuller
      Untitled Epic Poem on the History
      of Industrialization

a unit answers a question

this is the unit's fifth attempt to complete this novel.

the unit builds one cooling room. then another. the heat of stagnation. a factory line and fault line in a meatpacking district. sentences collapse on the edges of callouses. chattel move in. organs move out. the unit is brainless. and stupid. and useless. and tender.

George tells the unit that *every character needs a hole they are driven to fill*. it is the filling that drives the novel. the characters drive toward meaning. towards meaning they drive an ending.

where is the hole in your story he asks the unit.

the unit replies. *why. in the cow's head.*

a stanza is a breach in the wall

and why Limpet asks Hog in the waiting room *must we think in disaster.*

they drink sugar sluggish with tea. animal vegetable stone. a breakroom for tender udders. a field for gossip and fatigue. painful joints. the missing lingers. two animals who hate. each other. are cruel and kind. masculine skin sullen with salt.

Limpet guts himself. offers disaster. désastre is catastrophe. calamity. is a disastro. a weary word comprised of *dis* and *astro.* here is a star. is desastre. is dezastruc. is ill-starred. and malaise.

Hog inhales sweet oxygen of tea. is prose and peony. offers nothing in return.

Limpet calves. *disaster is an ill-fated star* he muses. a meteor. a tender most dreadful thing. heralds an eerie message of misinformation. ancestors. herders and hunters. who graze the dark sky. with prescience. who see divine emails. pale portents. a warning. a thin scale of light. who see catastrophe. a disclosure. a calloused finger. pointing toward the united states of disaster.

a thousand apocalypses happen each day. but not all of them are meat.

an apocalypse invents grace. and a sin.
a poem is house or a window.
something dear to look at.

yes Hog opines. *but how can we truly know disastro* if the serpentine ramp is calming

nurture. enchanting. the desire for dirt. offal. blood. urine. feces. to place the killing at the window. to graze sill while the unhappiness unfolds.

Limpet knows he has the right to suffer. to ask the awful question.

does your life have meaning?

Limpet sips his tea. a pinkie is pointing. he ages on skin. his fault line expanding. after ten years he finally replies.

who will rebuild that house?

a sentence is a feeding lair

a sentence is unit of things. a method for tension. an engine for world endings. a blank line. a house of disaster. an item of reflection. an accumulation of time. a conveyer belt. a meat hook. a design or a plan. a blueprint for factories. a list for contamination. letter grades. and percentages. credit or no credit. degree evaluations. employee numbers are pronouns. beef waste and urine. feces for fertiliser. satisfaction surveys. fresh clover. rancid student retentions. in this dumb world the sentence cages *your* sensitive intentions.

why is a house not a slaughterhome

because *we* will contribute nothing to a useful life.

The cow / is the continent // whose milk / (blood) is spilt. / What are we doing / with life? asks Vicuña.

this mesh of affinities is fragmented.

units are useful. downers are literal. monkey calves. paper sheep. the air is cupric and ferrous.

utility is glam. funk. futile. Limpet must make his living.

Limpet places the gun on a temple. a brain. a holy matter. ritual slaughter. mystic inscriptions on skin. a beautiful harrow.

Limpet is narrative and useless.

function he muses *is the is.*

does your life have meaning?

a difference.
that mark of.
indifference.

a house of laughter

many energies shape the field says Duncan. metaphor is militant. syntax demands the reorder of parts. a cow is a part in a system. also a poet. also mad brain. also a whole. also a cow is a moon. also meat. something that jumps over. this cow is milk. that cow is kind and kin. also kyne and capital. which is to say cattle and chattel. which is to say a metaphor. this sentence is sin.

today a tree is pungent with air. a day. one year. tomorrow a corral promotes soft waivers. of dust. hunger for rumour and furniture. the verdant urf demands the redness of authority. green capital withholds. hot hesitation. *you* live for movements. hours. and itineraries. *you* stand by the door. *you* wait for the fantasy of heaven. *what kind of worker are you?* withdraw *your* labour. refuse the demands for retention. tourists crushed by the slant of laughter like. blunt objects in the blunt structure of feeling. intelligence is for birds. some birds. not others. one to like is once to liken. one transfer to another. a carry over. two parts to a whole gathers ill feeling.

papier-mâché

Limpet is certain he can revise Grandin's design. he will create an oikos of dirt. urine. paper sheep. monkey calves. a public commons of ligature. an antithesis of blood and water. a dark pastoral for organs. a house without control. a commons of learning. an unreasonable college.

he designs a house with laughter.
then he designs a house with horror.

he designs a house with networks.
he designs a house with walls insulated with grief.
he designs a house with floors on the ceiling.
he designs a house with lairs and cold storage.
he designs a house with sponges and murals.
he designs a house with gestures. glass and mirrors.
he designs a house of steam and silk.
he designs a house of clover and trees.
he designs a house of syntaxes.
he designs a house of letters.
he designs a house of fences.
he designs a house without enclosures.
he designs a house of jargon. slang and cliché.
he designs a house of imperfection.
he designs a house with terrible teaching.
he designs a house without evaluations.
he designs a house without failure to meet. meets. or exceeds expectations.
he designs a house without walls and windows.
he designs a house without slogans.
he designs a house without building better communities of learning.
he designs a house without excellence.
he designs a house with wild gardens.
he designs a house with torture.
he designs a house without teaching awards.
he designs a house without high impact learning.

he designs a house without quality matters.
he designs a house without meetings.
he designs a house without enrollment.
he designs a house with access.
he designs a house with poetry.
he designs a house with brave rooms and hardship.
he designs a house without publish and perish.
he designs a house that never compels to *thank you for understanding*.
he designs a house that asks him *does your life have meaning?*

a unit wrestles with this narrative

this is the unit's twelfth attempt to write this novel.

the unit complains to a friend. *the I is stuck.* stagnant. *a barnacle on this project.* the unit holds a pen an inch above the paper. when the hand disappears. the sentences are erased. repetitively the unit writes *the line is a unit in tension* as if to break the conditional. the poem is an abattoir. a slaughterhouse. a meatpacking plant. a butcher. a dock street. a stockyard. a synonym for displeasure. the narrative is a corral in a loop. saturated with metaphors. to write the animal life is to write from a distance. the unit stands in its yard and bellows in anger.

the neighbours open their curtains. the neighbours close their curtains. the neighbours enclose in a pen. the neighbours are watching for slogans and excellence. the unit will record the time of its death. smoke o'clock. prosopopoeia cuts from the sick heat of labour. all is left is ritual surrender.

the unit slips into a car and drives to the city. the city is a line. a narrative for mourning. the first half of the sun is grit. and the second promises a difference. the city is a factory for organising indifference. the unit hits a cow who has wandered onto the road. together these meats drive to a college. they have tea fattened with sugar and milk. they see a student-led show before quietly dying. already this narrative is too taxing and trite. the plot is in debt. after their deaths the unit buries the cow in the backyard. and waits for inspiration. after six years it resurrects from the dirt with a PhD. applies for jobs with professionalised CVs. writes cover letters with keywords. research agendas. teaching philosophies. portfolios. writing samples. drops pronouns for ritual slaughter.

a unit is inspected

a beautiful disassembly line of cars and cattle. a division of labour. sharp knives cut limbs and hooves. from corral to knock box. skinning line to headline. gut able to tripe box. to tongue chain. boxcars. refrigerators. and supermarkets. a factory of narration. one line follows another. and another. then another. and another. an architect of cows and bolts. writer's block a harrow waiting for mystic inscription. meat on the corral. meat in the doors. meat in the stalls. the killing floor. walking meat in a classroom. meat in faculty meetings. meat in tenure reviews. meat in job interviews. meat in evaluations. another article. another poem. another book project. another product. another useful body part. another ghost institution who *thanks you for understanding*. competition is a cut in the hand. a limb trussed up. even the text crumples. the vessel exsanguinates. inspected. found tubercular with whiteness. a poxed brain. a desk reject. a revise and resubmit. the result is decline. a mad cow. sorry another downer.

a novel design

Limpet designs a novel idea. a harrow to be *a field of teaching excellence*. a machine for ritual execution. a bed of cotton and needles that pricks awe onto bare skin. six hours of pain. he predicts. then six hours of inspiration. twelve hours to execute in terrible derangement. an ill-starred omen. a malaise. a sense of disappointment. feces. blood. urine. and manure that mask the dull pain. glass walls and ceilings. no floors. no thresholds. this is a system of contamination. to witness is to bear an invisible burden. to disrupt cellular sanitation. to grade. and review. to assign standardisation. to bear the sentient text that *thanks you for understanding*. to withhold the travesty of counting. the economy of telling. a rigid narration.

Limpet designs his machine with her singular desire.

he is mad. insane. and demented.

he designs the harrow to discipline and perish and publish and punish.

two animals argue between their meats on the killing floor

light travels virtually in the red morning sun. bitterness is the gravity of longing. if the grass is blue. it is also kind. kindness demands the concretion of rigour. love is capillary action. consumes the exacting. particles of water are dirt and stomach. a hunger for production and organs. vibrations of prey are molten or glass. age mates of another species. a kinship with salutations of whales. Limpet tests his pronouns. he has to make his killing.

we are whales. Limpet rabbits Hog. stuns another unit.

Hog stomachs a neck. *we are beef.* he replies. *lean meat.*

we are larks. Limpet whales Hog.
we are entanglements of organs.

we are sparrows.
we are lungs and hearts.
we ae leeches or slugs.
we are bladders and lard.
we are tapeworms or sharks.
we are glands. kneecaps. skulls and spleens.

who is speaking? the unit wonders. *who is the voice in this system?*

dear lord give us the grace of a dean. Limpet leeches to no one in particular.

and the leech replies. *does your life have meaning?*

a unit shows discomfort

this is the unit's fifteenth attempt to write this novel.

the unit uncovers thresholds and sentiment. not heavens and corrals. in its text the cow jumps over the moon.

what you learn in school is that the kid next to you is your enemy writes Rubin. *love is impossible.*

to study means to be with other people writes the KUNCI Study Forum & Collective.

don't learn to do writes Butler. *but learn in doing.*

where is the power that controls your life here writes Rich.

this text is awkward as a crutch on a cow. the narrative is guts and shallow. the unit chews the cud and the cusp. the cut and the text. the unit despairs and sorrows. the unit has not learned how to jump over the moon. but the moon has jumped over the unit.

a unit designs a novel house

a garden of thistles and biddy bids. the rage of cicadas droning in trees. a mystical inscription machine in the lungs of a grove. doorways of pinewood and old clover. rose thorn and sweet bramble. an unreasonable college buds on the edge of the city. a mission for Madness. disastrous inquiry. a wound of infinitives. a bruise of prefixes. a gash of suffixes. gerunds and pluperfects. continuous presents. the unit is imagining a perfect future. helpfully burns ludicrous textbooks too expensive for purchase. secular classrooms. poor skin and useful for slaughter.

the unit creates an education of angles. hurts. and discomfort. builds a strange house of imperfect assembly. green air. parks. the canopy levels pollination. pollution. and disagreement. here the unreasonable house is a college of unreason. useless faculty poll for enchantment. understanding. *you* are bewildered. *you* circulate in air. a primitive question flounders. *unreason is part of reason* writes Butler. what speculation is. is contained in the verb. offing unveils a pause upon the gentle stranger's sentence.

the unit converses in a hypothetical language. *the classroom* says hooks *is a radical space of possibility*. words without transgression rewards commodification. banal radicalism couched in the guffaw of capitalism. but for its innovation in predictable practice a unit is awarded an endowed chair. critical imagination is recalled in the passive. the unit is now a *professor of inconsistency and evasion*. time to celebrate. time to profit. unbox those books. it can now write modern poetry.

the brochure is colour

you mask the whiteness *by changing the image* writes Ahmed. the mother vetoes change. papier-mâché. cotton sheep. a complaint. a biography of negation. a bad blockage. a no with a cut. a knife. some tears are more pleasurable than others. *a promise of happiness.* a promise of patience. *you* cannot separate the mother from the wiring.

her use is abuse. obtuse. noose. misuse. produce. profuse. overuse. reuse. ballyhoos. the mother's no is not the child's no.

what does not change is the will to change reminds Olson this line furthers inquiry.

what does not change is a resistance to change. because *you* are a beautiful resource.

Limpet loves doorways. they are slow to open. they are firm to close. the way they are left ajar. he hovers at the doorway. she edges her foot in. he shakes the handle. she sips sugar with tea. he knocks on the door. she dips the steam with bread. together they whisper in the dark.

a unit attends a workshop

a colleague asks what is *your* blue door.

no cries Limpet. he is finally uncomfortable.

this abattoir is a college

a can of spameducation

is a purposeful mecha. a unit of windows and doorways to heaven. a ledge of stars. and constellations. spells and enchantment. a college that is a loss of. lips of. desire and pain. *academic freedom* is *connected to* strange kinds of *commodity.* imprints of consumer. albatrosses to the slaughter. an abattoir of. productivity. quality. safety. transparency. inhumanity. bureaucracy. the *purpose [of education] should be to lead the mind to heights of understanding* argues Williams. thus. inclusivity. difficulty and excellence arrive at the slaughterhouse. in this abattoir the units relearn the felt of their fingers. fabrication and disassembly replace one concentric system for another. family is a glum word for employment. forced company is a slogan. is this a community or a committee. remember. the institution is a mother.

she will never love *you* back.

a unit is perishable in the slaughterhome

the unit must finish the novel.
the unit must teach a class.
the unit must revise an essay.
the unit must draft a proposal.
the unit must say no at appropriate times.
the unit must serve on the committee.
the unit must stun the unit.
the unit must serve on the committee.
the unit must serve on the committee.
the unit must serve on the committee.
the unit must write the assignments.
the unit must scaffold the assignments.
the unit must serve on that committee.
the unit must hold office hours.
the unit must attend a meeting.
the unit must attend a meeting.
the unit must enter the ramp.
the unit must teach a class.
the unit must grade the assignments.
the unit must serve on the committee.
the unit must write a grant.
the unit must revise the essay.
the unit must write the review.
the unit must submit an abstract.
the unit must ask for an extension.
the unit must attend a meeting.
the unit must attend a meeting.
the unit must walk down the corral.
the unit must teach a class.
the unit must teach a class.
the unit must attend a meeting.
the unit must write the essay.
the unit must submit an abstract.
the unit must grade the assignment.
the unit must revise the essay.
the unit must revise the essay.
the unit must submit the essay.
the unit must attend a meeting.
the unit must serve on the committee.
the unit must teach a class.
the unit must write a grant.
the unit must finish the novel.
the unit must revise the essay again.
the unit must stun that unit.
the unit must attend the conference.
the unit must network.
the unit must grade the assignment.

this abattoir is a college

the unit must grade the assignment.
the unit must submit an abstract.
the unit must walk down the corral.
the unit must attend a meeting.
the unit must teach a class.
the unit must attend the conference.
the unit must finish the novel.
the unit must serve on the committee.
the unit must write a grant.
the unit must grade the assignments.
the unit must stun the unit.
the unit must grade the assignment.
the unit must submit the essay.
the unit must serve on the committee.
the unit must attend a meeting.
the unit must submit an abstract.
the unit must grade the assignments.
the unit must submit a proposal.
the unit must write a grant.
the unit must attend a meeting.
the unit must teach a class.
the unit must serve on the committee.
the unit must do the assignment.
the unit must finish the assignments.
the unit must submit an abstract.
the unit must attend the conference.
the unit must read the essay.
the unit must serve on the committee.
the unit must teach a class revision.
the unit must devise the syllabus.
the unit must serve on the committee.
the unit must submit the assignments.
the unit must submit the proposal.
the unit must write the committee.
the unit must write the committee.
the unit must serve on the committee.
the unit must submit abstract.
the unit must serve on the committee.
the unit must attend a meeting.
the unit must schedule meeting.
the unit must teach a class.
the unit must serve on the committee.
the unit must grade the assignment.
the unit must submit the essay.
the unit must attend a class.
the unit must teach the essay.
the unit must walk down the corral.
the unit must submit the committee.
the unit must finish the novel.
the unit must serve on the committee.
the unit must finish the assignments.
the unit must grade the assignment.
the unit must walk down the corral.
the unit must grade the assignment.
the unit must serve on the committee.
the unit must serve on the committee.
the unit must submit at appropriate times.
the unit must submit the revision.
the unit must finish the novel.
the unit must attend a meeting.
the unit must write the committee.
the unit must grade the proposal.
the unit must finish the abstract.
the unit must serve on the committee.
the unit must write the assignment.
the unit must submit the revision.
the unit must finish the committee.
the unit must grade the assignments.
the unit must write the abstract.
the unit must grade the assignment.
the unit must finish the assignments.
the unit must attend a meeting.
the unit must grade the assignments.
the unit must serve on the committee.
the unit must attend a meeting.
the unit must finish the assignments.
the unit must grade the assignments.
the unit must serve on the committee.
the unit must network.
the unit must write the essay.
the unit must attend a meeting.
the unit must network.
the unit must serve on the committee.
the unit must teach a class.
the unit must attend a meeting.
the unit must enter the ramp.
the unit must finish the assignments.
the unit must stun that unit.
the unit must attend a meeting.
the unit must revise the essay.
the unit must walk down the corral.
the unit must attend a meeting.

the unit must serve on a committee. the unit must grade these papers. the unit must prepare for a class. the unit must respond to an email. the unit must counsel a student. the unit must advise a student.

this abattoir is a college

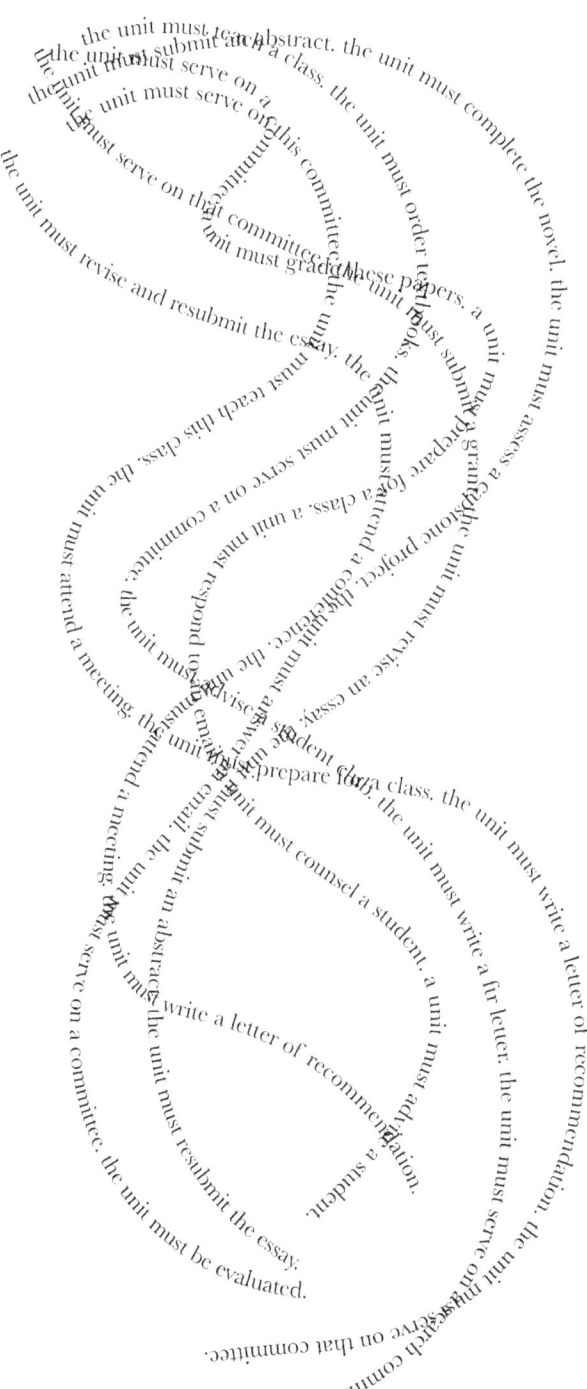

the unit must teach a class. the unit must complete the novel. the unit must submit an abstract. the unit must order papers. a unit must assess a student. the unit must serve on a committee. the unit must serve on this committee. the unit must submit a grant. the unit must prepare for a class. a unit must revise an essay. the unit must attend a conference. the unit must advise a student. the unit must write a letter of recommendation. the unit must serve on this committee. the unit must serve on that committee. the unit must graduate. the unit must teach this class. the unit must respond to an email. the unit must advise a student. the unit must prepare for a class. the unit must write a fir letter. the unit must write a letter of recommendation. the unit must research. the unit must serve on that committee. the unit must revise and resubmit the essay. the unit must attend a meeting. the unit must send an email. the unit must submit an abstract. the unit must advise a student. the unit must serve on a committee. the unit must write a letter of recommendation. the unit must counsel a student. a unit must advise a student. the unit must resubmit the essay. the unit must be evaluated.

no.

a pedagogy of enchantment

why is a semester a semester wonders Limpet. a quarter a quarter. why is a fifty-minute class a tactical session. why three hours not four. why is the structure a closure. a pen holding slaughter. a blue door to heaven.

Limpet designs a pedagogy of enchantment. a spell. a chant. a magical prayer. an insistence on unreason. irrationality. and madness. a system for hypothetics. and critical sadness. flummoxed forms gather in empty hallways and open doors.

o o o o o o Limpet realises.

poetry is the poverty line.

but can it dissolve the mother.

...reference...tion.
Are as far as H the same as in the plan excepting
only F which does not appear.

| I Annular cistern for water to supply every cell. | ...s for keeping provisions tools, materials | to ventilate the whole building when opened. |
| K Rooms serving for lodging the tuskmasters, inspectors | L Large annular skylight serving | M Skylight to the Chapel. N.O Parts not yet applied to any use. |

Plan of House of Inspection.

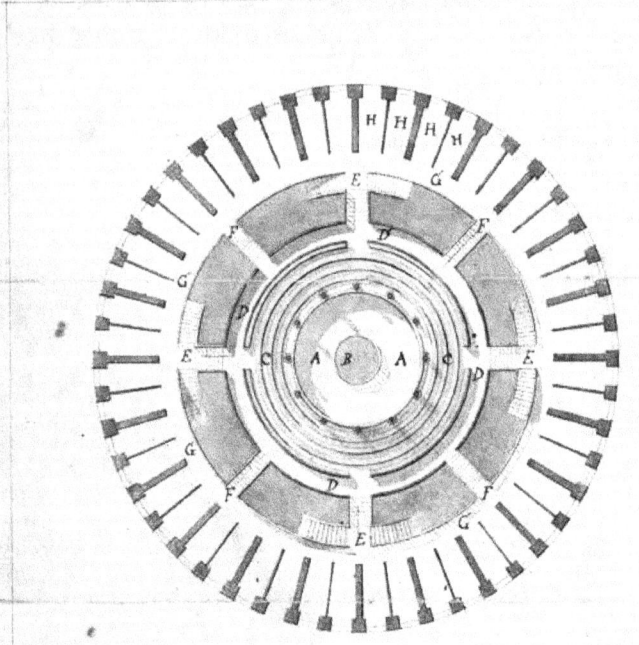

10 20 30 40 50 60   10 ft

References on this Plan.

- A —
- A Chapel.
- B Circular opening to light the storys underneath.
- C Gallery of the chapel.
- D Inspector's Gallery
- E Semi staircases leading from bottom to top of the building, & from one story of the cells to the inspectors gallery.
- F Communications from the same to the other story of cells.
- G Gallery of general communication for the cells.
- H Cells, two of which may be laid into one.

desire

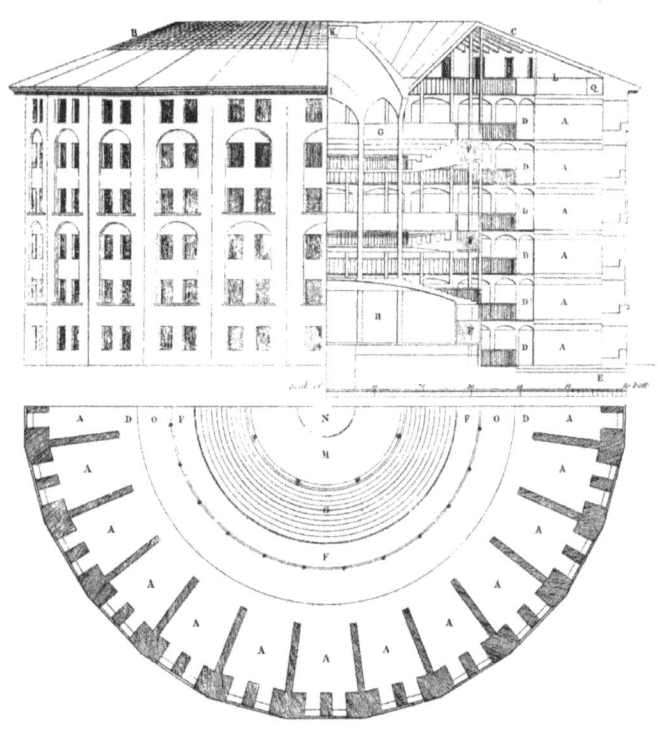

What could the city—as a network of layered relationships and an assemblage of histories—offer and afford in studying solidarity?
—KUNCI Study Forum & Collective,
Letters: The classroom is burning, let's dream about a School of Improper Education

you want me to tell you the marvels of invention?
that we persevere
 that the time of flourishing is at hand?
—*D.A. Powell*, "republic"

To teach a boy to open his eyes to these possibilities, and so to prepare him for all sorts of emergencies, is the object of this system of hypothetics. To imagine a set of utterly strange and impossible contingencies, and require the youths to give intelligent answers to the questions that arise therefrom, is reckoned the fittest conceivable way of preparing them for the actual conduct of their affairs in after life.
—Samuel Butler, *Erewhon*

a slaughterhouse for spameducation

this narrative is cloven

this is the unit's thirtieth attempt to write this novel.

this is an image inverted. this is a community. a place for fatality. this is an abattoir. the largest in the city. this is a haunt on the banks of a river. this is a spectre of dread. a zombie of toil. this is a century that calls itself dust.

this is a building next to the train station. this is a man made of red lungs and grey meat. this is a man who calls himself Martin. Martin is a man with a vision for a system. he prizes efficiency and white sanitation. he is an artist and a machinist. a foreman and a manager. Martin is an inventor of an all-in-one harrow. here he murders. here he enchants. here he builds a façade of limestone and widgets. here he erects the sublime onto terracotta. here he weaves his lust into high fire brick. he swells his desire into reinforced concrete.

there on the roof the cattle observe. the trains arrive. more units disembark. this roof is a dead zone for waiting. when tourists move in. organs depart. the city surrenders to the regime of fresh meat. there is a line. there is a ramp. carcasses congeal on the floor. there Martin delights in the stickiness of killing. there the units are dismantled into different heaps. offal and limbs. hearts and livers. kidneys and hides. fat and tongues wash the basement.

this house. can hold. many fertile strangers. this house is an abattoir and an upholstery store. this house is a headquarters for a supermarket. shelters a newspaper. this space is a lattice of red brick and grey beef. a cover of clover and cleaver. monkey calves. and paper sheep. when the unit photographs this house. an Irish Pub has moved onto the street-level floor. what awes the unit is not the beer. the drunks. the two-piece suits. but a sign on the wall that crows *Kaplan Education Institute*. learning is burning and SATs are now the cows' knees. all-in-one histories move from bone and grist to college dreams and for-profit test preps.

Limpet realises he has built a college

and becomes a professor.

Hog becomes a dean.

here the classroom is hierarchy. here a sentence. here a cut in the hand for half-a-pencil. here units go in. here grades go out. here he lectures. here he listens. here he takes notes. here he shuffles the alphabet. he writes letters of recommendation and post-tenure reviews. he drafts evaluations. he receives evaluations. he is a wound for evaluation. here he teaches. here he serves. here he builds an arc for narration. here is his hole. he dresses in ribbons.

you ought to be grateful

because *you* have a job.

because *you* are a beautiful resource.

a pedagogy of enchantment is a mouthful of no.

remember Hog writes into the handbook. *the institution will never love* you *back.*

to profess demands confession

Limpet attends a professional development workshop where he knits slogans of wellbeing.

forget official verse culture Limpet cries. *we're living in an official working culture.*

an official college culture.

an official pedagogy culture.

Limpet needs to think. she needs to linger slowly.

you must cross the genre of pedagogy.

teach teach muses Limpet.

profess profess profess.

confess confess confess.

incite incite incite.

enchant enchant enchant.

idle idle idle beyond the line.

Limpet receives an email

dear professor dear colleague dear mr limpet hey dear faculty hi dear dr limp dear lump a meeting is scheduled this unit is sick projectile vomiting on the toilet faculty reviews are due grandpa grandma auntie uncle dog cat died broke up with a girlfriend boyfriend best friend thank *you* a review has shattered the global order of everyday life what can the unit do to catch up did the unit miss anything important please send in a progress report covid covid covid why are students arriving late to class the unit is on conditional enrolment employment sorry this unit has missed the meeting covid covid thank *you* for *your* patience this unit needs a letter of recommendation for off campus study an internship a job ma mfa phd programme college transfer thank *you* the unit loves the class with covid brain fog when is the assignment due the review letter due when is the meeting here is a resume a cv need a grade boost just point five will do to swing the unit towards an A an exceeds expectations do *you* need accommodations thank *you* climate change rally and people are dying thank *you* please sign this petition please sign *this* petition how can *you* can teach when there is a war genocide hurricane tornado school shooting happening thank *you* can *you* bump up the participation grade please chair this committee congratulations on *your* recent publication *your* article grant application has been rejected *you* must provide a letter of recommendation thank *you* covid the unit appreciates *your* service please join this steering committee advisory committee standing committee learning community interest group thank *you* please donate *your* blood donate *your* old magazines donate *your* time donate a portion of *your* salary to support students staff in need thank *you* we're hiring please join us for a meditation hour thank *you* covid sick flu coughing uploading the resume now sick and on the toilet again the unit didn't submit the assignment review letter but will do so today tomorrow sometime next week maybe after the semester this unit cannot come to this class meeting appointment today sorry the unit forgot but who knows time is a construct and depression is acid an abattoir a cow fit for the slaughter sorry sorry sorry to be a downer

thank *you* for understanding.

a unit creates a curriculum for its unreasonable college

an immodest proposal

community service for improper values.
the poetics of the commons.
the study of three languages.
the fourth language is fictional.
hypothetics.
critical irrationality.
a course in bubble studies.
read any book and think *bodily* about it.
select a poem *you* love and *appreciate* it.
a course on beekeeping.
a course on urban and rural farming in response to climate change.
absolutely no courses.
discomfort.
the poetics of this discomfort.
what capitalism demands. the politics of idleness or how *we* can be useless.
saying no to requests.
withdrawal is not a surrender.
planting for pollinators.
solar energetics.
the subaltern of three lashings.
against similes.
assembling anarchist identities for socialist plants.
students are not units. a colouring book against capital.
physics. poetry. and the mystical arts of engineering.
read "The Book of the Dead" by Muriel Rukeyser.
read *The Charm and the Dead* by Rodrigo Toscano.
read *labor* by Jill Magi.
read *General Motors* by Ryan Eckes.
read "the Abomunist Manifesto" by Bob Kaufman.
read *Coal Mountain Elementary* by Mark Nowak.
read "The classroom" by Audre Lorde.
read "A Different Way of Talking" by Patricia Grace.

read "No Ordinary Sun" by Hone Tuwhare.
read

assessment is the chalk. a writ in the dirt.

you are a belly of no.

*Limpet strikes a manifesto for learning
at an unreasonable college*

because *we* will contribute to a useless life. find joy in the fallow. without value for capital.

abandon the employee number Limpet declares. be a comparison without metaphor. decide *your* own punishment. without citizenships and transactions.

mentorship is built on an implicit hierarchy that you should be suspicious of writes Firestone.

Limpet recites. unites. incites with erratic satellites.

how would the most privileged among us so easily ascend academia to outrank survivors and working-class peasants if we abandoned the decorum of professionalized poetry discourse in a university setting? reflects Melgard.

as the world changes, so do our ways of living it and this must be reflected in how students learn reasons kaufman.

where is intention ponders Limpet. *where is slow education.* Limpet wants to idle. laze. absorb. think. he desires a limb of error.

universities are a *repository of knowledge and expertise. they accept a role as critic and conscience of society* reminds the unit's homeland law. the university is not a parking lot. not a monument. not a strip mall. not a cvs pharmacy.

the university is *[a]n institution of higher learning, consisting of an assemblage of colleges united under one corporate organization and government, affording instruction in the arts and sciences and the learned professions, and confers degrees* declares Hog. his finger reads the dictionary.

the university is a contradiction. a prison. a tool for capital. for patents. and machines.

when your life has no meaning. Limpet writes in his blank notebook. the empty pen anchors the paper.

the solution is

this is not a metaphor

Limpet attends the MLA. he waits for his session. he scours the conference for a free seat. he sits at a table. he charges his laptop. he revels in dirt. he showers with beef. he drinks artificial sugar sickened with tea. a pod of three poets arrive. they sit at the next table. he listens sublimely while they share their wet burgers.

if you are high enough in orbit says one *you can still see the pyramids.*

if you travel from urf says another *you can watch their construction.*

if the sun disappears we could live for eight minutes.

everything they agree *comes down to the light.*

and Hejinian inquires *isn't the avant-garde always pedagogical?*

Limpet leaves his table. he searches the hotel for a stupid man's name. he finds the strange man and the cold room is empty. two scholars arrive. two scholars depart. the AV system rejects his beautiful presentation. murmurs and heartbeats. clover and cleaver. he hears a soft voice behind a blue door. *I grew up impoverished* it says. *I was middle class.* another unit appears. and organs depart. this unit is disassembled for internal inquiry.

when it is his turn to speak Limpet misreads his paper. he pauses dramatically at unimportant moments. *academics are not wrong to fear the poets* says Silliman. everyone laughs. but one unit grieves. Limpet concludes his paper with a question because he likes final provocations. when a unit applauds *does your life have meaning?* there is a killing at the window. organs move out. skeletons remain. Limpet chews his mouth. knows he has the right to suffer. when he looks up from the podium the room is barren. even his organs have departed.

Limpet sits down with his hands on his lap. pricks his skin on the holy harrow. how far into space need he be to watch this *disaster* again.

again he muses.

and again.

and again.

Limpet laughs to himself. a capital joke.

yes. yes. yes. yes he cries.

you will do it again.

useful and used up

there is a strange burning in *your* belly. salt and chalking. use is. limed. and brined. a mass. a mess. wasted and queer. on his heels the soul is tread and trod. garbaged and grotesque. a blister of no. a burst of liver. stasis. brain mist. if *you* open the door. lie on the threshold. guard *your* desire. hold a no to *your* chest. sip *your* beef tea. veto the dark. assemble in the threshold. close *your* door if *you* must.

how can you teach a successful poem

Limpet writes a poem on the whiteboard.
Limpet bruises the poem on the white whiteboard.

here is a process of time he reminds the class. *a poem is about this unknowing.* Limpet pauses dramatically. he unties his shoelaces slowly. his fault line is fumbling quietly.

a poem is an invitation he guesses. *and a line is a unit of thought.*

Limpet writes these sceptical words on the white white whiteboard. carefully he ties his laces.

poetry holds with open arms writes Piombino. Limpet unties his laces.

Limpet narrates and edits a journal. he holds one-on-one conversations. he mentors young poets. he creates different zines. he hosts weird readings in living rooms. in theatres. and on college lawns. he chalks poems on pavements and on post office walls. he emails a stranger that simply says *love you*. and slowly he ties his white white white shoelaces.

to the class Limpet reads the poem aloud. units click their fingers. slowly he unties his laces.

your reading needs shape prods Silliman. Limpet quickly unties his laces. he mouths a mad mantra. he entices enchantment. he hums. a serpentine ramp is calming.

what poets write is less interesting than their silences counters Limpet. he ties his laces. he lies. and writes on his skin. he recites and unites and incites and delights. Sharp claims *the industrialization of literature is a churning word factory.*

but a poem is about feelings. fingers click violently. Limpet shivers. he weeps. he points to the slaughterhome of history.

education is [...] *an offence against freedom of thought* argues Krenak.

Limpet is used. refused. and abused. a mineral resource for extraction.

o o o o o Limpet finally cries.
and he teaches *this abattoir is a college.* at last he yells.
let the poet's novel corrupt *you.*

unleashed Limpet ties his shoelaces. he burns down the classroom. he unties his dirty laces.

he burns down the classroom.

he burns down the classroom.

he burns down the classroom.

the students untie their laces.

Limpet cultivates a countersyllabus

how to be useless or used less

withdraw *your* arm. let it weaken in mass.

course texts. there are no required texts. everything is required. find a poem *you* love. read it on a train. or on a park bench. in bed. under a tree. on a busy street. start in media res. or at the end. it does not pay to flatter the poet. hate them. or hate them. resist the poem's object. physical copies only. e-copies only. no copies. create the poem *yourself*. if hungry eat the words. the stanzas will provide shelter.

assignments. communicate what *you* don't know. share *your* observations like marbles. gift string to *your* peers. play cats eyes on the manhole covers. do not hoard *your* winnings. teach the unknown poem. invite the poet on the poverty line.

grade scale. none. the options are disgust. disappointment. discomfort. be reckless with enchantment. *we* are the tramp on the assembly line.

citation style. acknowledge *your* community. acknowledge *your* strangers. gift them grain on the Polaroid. marbles or foibles.

communication policy. tear a page from *your* notebook. write down *your* question in ink. bury *your* note in a discussed coffee cup. discard in the trash. watch a custodian collect it. gather the trash from them. pay them as faculty. gift them *your* marbles. expect nothing in return.

academic honesty. ChatGPT will honestly tell *you* what *you* think *you* know. the unit knows nothing.

classroom. an enclosure. exit onto the polluted street. visit a park or the urban garden. sit in a field or a park bench or an encampment. let the poem draw *you* to a world outside of itself. like it. poetry is a series of complex relations between word and context. perhaps this is politics.

pedagogical practice. *in the centrifugal classroom the teacher cannot function as the dispenser of wisdom, the class as a whole may not move toward consensus, and the individual reader* […] *may not move toward certainty* verbs Keller.

forget the student-centred classroom. it is time for a an idle-centred classroom. *you* need time to think. resist the life they intend for *you*.

Limpet's lesson plan is an idle arm

in *your* daily life recite.

        the institution is not a mother.

in *your* daily life answer.

        what makes *you* anxious.
        what defines *your* joy.
        are *you* happy.
        what makes *you* sad.
        what wisdom do *you* bring.
        what lines do *you* skew.
        what bones are lodged in *your* throat.
        what kinship can *you* make.
        how will *you* listen.
        are *you* happy.
        what spirit words speak to *you*.
        how does *your* body feel. next to a tree. on the street. on a bench.
        do *you* meander from one class to another.
        what do *you* notice on the path. the flower bed. the pavement.
        do *you* have enough money for the parking meter.
        what books do *you* read. what zines from which class.
        do *you* defy the desire for credentials.
        do *you* care.
        are *you* late to class.
        what did *you* learn from a stranger.
        what does the custodian say when *you* toss *your* cup.
        do *you* acknowledge them.
        do *you* help them clean up.
        do *you* carry the trash.
        do *you* wonder about its infrastructure.

what knowledge do they share with *you*.
do *you* cook *your* meals at the dining hall.
have *you* acknowledged your ancestors.
have *you* conversed with your descendants.
do *you* feed *your* peers in line.
what service do *you* offer others.
are *you* masked.
are *you* vaccinated.
are *you* sick in bed.
what is *your* duty of care.
who cares for *you*.
what are *your* obligations to learning.
what are *your* obligations to share.
do *you* have time to think.
can *you* relate.
do *you* relate.
do *you* need to relate.
do *you* find pleasure in difference.
are *you* idle.
are *you* in crisis.
who can help *you*.
are *you* happy for others.
are *you* happy for others.
are *you* happy.
are *you* happy.
are *you* useless.
are *you* useless.
are *you* useless.

are *you* useless?

there is a dead body under this draft

this is the unit's twentieth attempt to write this novel.

the fault of the "youth" lies […] *with those to whom it has been asked to look: to its elders, the leaders, the professors, who* […] *know next nothing at all* says Williams.

the right way to cure burnout is to kill the gun says Hog.
but who put the gun in the unit's hand Limpet replies.

a chorus of adages

every character needs a hole.
the history of women is the history of waiting.
does *your* life have meaning?
let the reader read beyond the page.
let the poem know a history.
the student is the theatre.
where is *your* community.
learning is recursive.
is this real.
what is real life.
every charlady needs a hologram.
fortification is never more than the extract of contingency.
what is *your* blue door.
the hoax of woodlands is the hoax of waiting.
let the reaper read beyond the pain.
what are *you* doing with *your* likeness.

the handbook for hard lists

create your own offer of tenure suggests Magi.

no / one listens to poetry writes Spicer. remember. the institution is a mother. who will never love *you* back.

Limpet creates a vacuum into which he hurts nouns. answers. solutions. innovation. hearts. radicalism. collaboration. student-centred learning. excellence. diversity. kidneys. inclusivity. hides. proposals. brains. grants. rumen. research. teaching. administration. bible. academic presses. abstracts. departments. tripe. grades. processes. maw. articles. blood. curricula. liver. bone. peer-review. search committees. dossiers. grants. cvs. contracts. advising. adjunctification. vaps. professionalisation. agents. hooves. lips. LMS. and service.

Limpet lies on the harrow. places a stone on his head. inks a letter of tenure onto his bare skin. he shudders with disappointment. enchants with warm feces. blood. urine. and manure mask his dull pain.

thank you he says weeping. *I accept this dishonour.*

necropastoral

when the line is a city. it is a narrative for mourning. the first half of the sun is grit. the second promises indifference. the city is a college for organising persistence. the college is a committee. a learning community. and a police machine.

in the morning the units herd Limpet onto a lorry. slowly they drive to slaughter. this home is a pen or a cage for the cleaver. pomp and parades. a throne for the monarchy. banners are hung for this special graduation. Limpet is an angel for this royal occasion.

he descends from the trainer with cattle for slaughter. he joins the ramp. follows the curving line of the corral. he waves to the parents. he waves to the units. he waves to the camera. he waves to the buildings. he waves to the crowds. he waves to his colleagues. and he waves to Hog at the end of the line. the serpentine ramp is calming.

this space is a lattice of red brick and grey beef. a cover of clover and cleaver. monkey calves. and paper sheep. Irish beer. GREs and SATs. flesh and candy. sugar and blood. a stranger engrained on the Polaroid photo. a murmur. a memory in the stall and killing floor. Hog is a system for smiling. a hand for diplomas. a seat for many speeches. the beat of the pneumatic gun cuts through compressed air. feet stumble on the concrete. learned and inutile research is mixed with brain and sweetmeat. a unit is useless. it closes the door. a worker moves out. Limpet moves in. *oh oh oh oh* he cries. *o o o o o.* organs move out.

lie on the threshold. close the door if *you* must.

cartload

"Abattoir Design." *Nature* (1934): 455–56. https://doi.org/10.1038/134455c0. https://www.nature.com/articles/134455c0.pdf.

Ahmed, Sara. *What's the Use? On the Uses of Use.* Durham: Duke University Press, 2019.

Basko, Aaron. "Will the 'Enrollment Cliff' Help or Hurt Your Career?" *The Chronicle of Higher Education*. February 23, 2024. Accessed April 23, 2024. https://www.chronicle.com/article/will-the-enrollment-cliff-help-or-hurt-your-career.

Beauvoir, Simone de. "The Useless Mouths." In *The Useless Mouths, and Other Literary Writings*, translated by Liz Stanley and Catherine Naji, edited by Margaret A. Simons and Marybeth Timmerman, 11–87. Urbana: University of Illinois Press, 2014.

Bernstein, Charles. *Content's Dream. Essays 1975–1984.* Evanston: Northwestern University Press, 1985.

Black, Henry Campbell. *A Law Dictionary*. St. Paul, MN: West Publishing Co., 1910.

Browne, Laynie, and Noah Saterstrom. *The Poet's Novel as a Form of Defiance: Indeterminate Frame*. Higganum, CT: Kin Press, 2020.

Butler, Samuel. *The Note-Books of Samuel Butler.* Edited by Henry Festing Jones. London: Dutton, 1917.

---. *Erewhon and Erewhon Revisited*. London: Dent, 1959.

Derrida, Jacques. "Force De Loi: Le Fondement Mystique De L'Autorite." *Cardozo Law Review* 11, no. 5–6 (1990): 920–1046.

Duncan, Robert. "Transmissions. Passages 33." In *Robert Duncan: The Collected Later Poems and Plays*, edited by Peter Quartermain, 451–457. Los Angeles: University of California Press, 2014.

Education and Training Act 2020, https://www.legislation.govt.nz/act/public/2020/ 0038/latest/LMS202213.html#LMS202213.

Foucault, Michel, and Jay Miskowiec. "Of Other Spaces." *Diacritics* 16, no. 1 (1986): 22–27.

Fuller, R. Buckminister. *Untitled Epic Poem on the History of Industrialization.* New York: Simon and Schuster, 1962.

Gladman, Renee. *Plans for Sentences.* Seattle: Wave Books, 2020.

Golding, Alan. "American Poet-Teachers and the Academy." In *A Concise Companion to Twentieth-Century American Poetry*, edited by Stephen Fredman, 55–74. Malden, MA: Blackwell Publishing, 2005.

Goldman, Andrew. "Temple Grandin on Autism, Death, Celibacy and Cows." *New York Times Magazine*, April 12, 2013. Accessed October 10, 2024. https://www.nytimes.com /2013/04/14/magazine/temple-grandin-on-autism-death-celibacy-and-cows.html.

Hejinian, Lyn. *My Life and My Life in the Nineties.* Middletown, CT: Wesleyan University Press, 2013.

hooks, bell. *Teaching to Transgress: Education as the Practice of Freedom.* London: Routledge, 1994.

Kafka, Franz. "In the Penal Colony." In *The Metamorphosis, In the Penal Colony, and Other Stories: The Great Short Works of Franz Kafka*, translated by Joachim Neugrochel, 189–230. New York: Simon & Schuster, 2000.

kaufman, erica. *POETRY and PEDAGOGY, POETRY is PEDAGOGY, PEDAGOGY is POETRY, POETRY in PEDAGOGY…* n.p. eohippus labs, n.d.

Keller, Lynn. "Fffffalling with Poetry: The Centrifugal Classroom." In *Poetry and Pedagogy: The Challenge of the Contemporary*, edited by Joan Retallack and Juliana Spahr, 30–38. New York: Palgrave Macmillan, 2006.

Krenak, Ailton. *Life is Not Useful.* Translated by Jamille Pinheiro Dias and Alex Brostoff. Cambridge, UK: Polity, 2023.

KUNCI Study Forum & Collective. *Letters: The Classroom Is Burning, Let's Dream About A School of Improper Education.* New York: Ugly Duckling Presse.

la paperson. *A Third University is Possible.* Minneapolis. University of Minnesota Press, 2017.

Le Corbusier. *Towards A New Architecture.* Translated by Frederick Etchells. New York: Dover, 1986.

Lee, Paula Young. "Siting the Slaughterhouse: From Shed to Factory." In *Meat, Modernity, and the Rise of the Slaughterhouse,* edited by Paula Young Lee, 46–70. University of New Hampshire Press, 2008.

Lorde, Audre. "A Litany for Survival. *Poetry Foundation*, April 26, 2024. Accessed October 10, 2024. https://www.poetryfoundation.org/poems/147275/a-litany-for-survival.

Magi, Jill. *Labor.* New York: Nightboat Books, 2014.

---. "Teaching & Poetry: A Dialogue with Jennifer Firestone." *Poetry Foundation*, October 30, 2017. Accessed January 14, 2024. https://www.poetryfoundation.org/harriet-books/2017/10/teaching-poetry-a-dialogue-with-jennifer-firestone.

McSweeney, Joyelle. *The Necropastoral: Poetry, Media, Occults.* Ann Arbor. University of Michigan Press, 2014.

Melgard, Holly. "Echochambermusics: Notes Toward a Trauma-Informed Poetry Pedagogy." In *Read Me: Selected Works,* 284–96. New York: Ugly Duckling Presse, 2023.

Olson, Charles. "The Kingfishers." *Poetry Foundation.* Accessed October 10, 2024. https://www.poetryfoundation.org/poems/54310/the-kingfishers-56d234829d88a.

Piombino, Nick. "With Open Arms." *Fait Accompli.* May 14, 2003. Accessed October 10, 2024. https://nickpiombino.blogspot.com/2003/05/with-open-arms-writing-poetry-is.html.

Powell, D.A. "Republic." *Poetry* July (2008). Accessed October 10, 2024. https://www.poetryfoundation.org/poetrymagazine/poems/51164/republic.

Puckett. John, L. "Efficiency under One Roof: D.M. Martin Co.'s One-Size-Fits-All Slaughterhouse." *West Philadelphia Collaborative History.* Accessed January 22, 2024. https://collaborativehistory.gse.upenn.edu/stories/efficiency-under-one-roof-dm-martin-co's-one-size-fits-all-slaughterhouse.

Reading, Bill. *The University in Ruins*. Cambridge, MA: Harvard UP, 1998.

Rich, Adrienne. "Assignment for week of May 18: Jerry Rubin." *What we are part of. Part 1.* Edited by Iemanjá Brown, Stefania Heim, erika kaufman, Kristin Moriah, Conor Tomás Reed, Talia Shalev, Wendy Tronrud, and Ammiel Alcalay. New York: The Center for the Humanities, 2013.

Salaita, Steven. "The Inhumanity of Academic Freedom." *Third World Approaches to International Law Review.* November 2, 2020. Accessed October 11, 2024. https://twailr.com/the-inhumanity-of-academic-freedom/.

Sharp, Travis. *Behind the Poet Reading Their Poem is a Sign Saying Applause.* n.p. Knife Fork Book, 2022.

Silliman, Ron. "Unlearning to Write." In *Poets on Teaching: A Sourcebook*, edited by Joshua Marie Wilkinson. Iowa City: University of Iowa Press, 2010.

---. *Lit*. Potes & Poets Press, 1987.

Spicer, Jack. *The Collected Books of Jack Spicer*, edited by Robin Blaser. Los Angeles: Black Sparrow Press, 1975.

van der Zee, Bibi. "From School to the Slaughterhouse." *Guardian*, April 29, 2010. Accessed October 10, 2024. https://www.theguardian.com/lifeandstyle/ 2010/apr/29/school-farms-teaching-food-origins.

Vicuña, Cecilia . *Precario/precarious*. Translated by Anne Twitty. New York: Tanam Press, 1983.

Williams, William Carlos. *The Embodiment of Knowledge*. New York: New Directions, 1974.

workers whose voices echo through mine

to those who have helped this project either directly or indirectly, in one revision or another, thank you: Barbara Brookes. Simon Garcia. James George. Yutan Getzler. Katherine Hedeen. Michael Leong. Lisa Samuels.

to my colleagues who attended the manuscript workshop and offered critical feedback, I appreciate *you*: Alex Brostoff. Frances Cannon. Adele Davidson. Sarah Heidt. Jesse Matz. Alyssa Quinn. Sergei Lobanov-Rostovsky.

this is a field of labour

this project was first conceived and written on the traditional homelands of Ngāti Whātua, Kawerau ā Maki, Tainui, Ngāti Pāoa, Wai-O-Hua, and Ngāti Rehua. it began its life as a very different novel while I attended the MCW programme at the University of Auckland in 2009. its evolution is very much owed to the generous feedback from my cohort in Lisa Samuels' seminar. after numerous abortive attempts at revision, it was put aside for several years. I finally returned to the manuscript in 2019 following my relocation to Ohio. it was extensively revised on the traditional homelands of the Shawnee, Lenni Lenape, and Osage peoples, who are very much still here and thriving.

an early portion of this manuscript was published as *blue doors: excerpts from a failed novel* with Belladonna* Press in 2018.

versions of *a stanza is a breach in the wall*, *two animals argue between their meats on the killing floor*, and *the college is a managed pastoral* appeared in rob mclennan's *touch the donkey*, issue 26, 2020.

and, lastly, thank you dd white and Calamari Archive, Ink for taking a chance with this weird book.

orchid tierney is a poet and scholar from Aotearoa New Zealand. she is the author of the collection *a year of misreading the wildcats* (The Operating System, 2019) and several chapbooks: *pedagogies of the planthroposcene* (above/ground press, forthcoming), *looking at the Tiny: Mad lichen on the surfaces of reading* (Essay Press, 2023), *my beatrice* (above/ground press, 2020), *ocean plastic* (BlazeVOX Books, 2019), and *blue doors: excerpts from a failed novel* (Belladonna* Press in 2018), among others. she teaches English at Kenyon College and is a senior editor at the *Kenyon Review.*
www.orchidtierney.com.

www.ingramcontent.com/pod-product-compliance
Lightning Source LLC
Chambersburg PA
CBHW070155080526
44586CB00015B/2004